ULTIMATE COMIC ART

DRAWING MONSTROUS HEROES

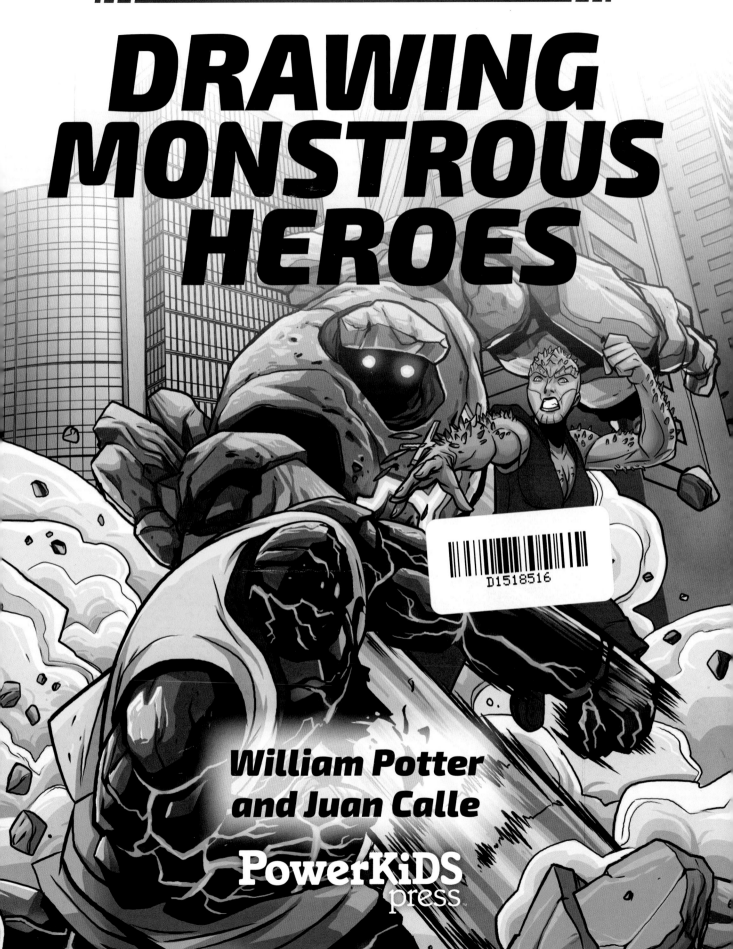

William Potter
and Juan Calle

PowerKiDS press

CONTENTS

HEROIC MONSTERS

Not every hero has to be human — sometimes heroic teams need someone a little more unusual! It's time to create some beastly heroes of your own!

LET'S MAKE COMICS

We're going to take inspiration from all over the place — nature, science, animals, and aliens — to create some fantastic characters. You don't have to be a great artist, just get started with a pencil and paper and see where the action takes you!

STEPS AHEAD

Monsters are great to draw as they can be made of anything, but they still need to be believable. Discover how to draw the mightiest, most monstrous menaces with guides to drawing exaggerated muscles, tough **TEXTURES**, dramatic lighting, and spooky scenarios. We'll look at body language and settings for your monsters, to make it all frighteningly realistic!

Get ready to meet some monsters! Here comes a band of crazy creatures just waiting to test out their superpowers in some spooktastic situations. Turn the page to meet them . . . if you dare . . .

GETTING STARTED

You don't need a desk full of expensive tools to start making comics. You just need a pen, some paper, and a wild imagination!

PENCILS

Drawing pencils come in various hardnesses. H pencils are harder and B pencils are softer. A 2H pencil is good for making light marks that don't smudge, while a 2B is good for sketching. Try using pencils of different hardnesses to find those you're most comfortable with. You'll need a sharpener and an eraser of course! You could also use a mechanical pencil.

CURVES

Drawing smooth curves for action lines and speech balloons can be tricky. A set of curves or a circle and ellipse template can help. For perfect circles, use a template or drawing compass.

PAPER

You can draw on any kind of paper, especially for early sketches and planning. For final drafts, professional comic artists use a thick, smooth art paper. Comics are drawn larger than they are printed in comic books.

PENS

Pens are a matter of personal choice. You might try out many different kinds before you find the perfect match. Find a pen that gives you a solid, permanent line. As you grow as a comic artist, you'll want to expand your pen collection. Eventually, you'll need pens of different thicknesses and a marker for filling in large areas.

BRUSHES, FOUNTAIN PENS

Inking over your pencils with a fountain pen or a brush dipped in ink will require some practice and a steady hand, but it can produce great results! A brush will give you more control over the thickness of your lines. Brushes are also good for filling in large areas with black ink that won't fade. You might also like working with brush pens.

STRAIGHT EDGES

You'll need a smooth metal or plastic ruler to draw comic panels and lines for comic book lettering. A triangle is also useful for panel drawing.

Many professional comic artists draw and color their art using tablets and computers. However, when you're just starting to learn and practice comic art skills, nothing beats good old pen and paper. You can get your ideas down while mastering basic techniques.

BODY MATTERS

When you can draw a figure with accurate proportions, your characters will look more realistic. Superheroes and villains often have exaggerated muscular physiques — some may even have animal or alien features!

TOP TIP
You don't have to give all of your comic book characters an athletic build. Use different heights and body shapes so that readers find it easier to tell them apart.

The human body is symmetrical, with the bones and muscles on the left matching those on the right.

Men's bodies are often wide at the shoulders and chests, then narrower at the hips. Women's bodies are often narrow at the waist and wider at the hips, like the number 8.

All human bodies are about eight heads tall. The waist is about three heads down from the top of the body, and the hands reach midway down the thigh.

When you draw a person standing up straight, you should be able to draw a straight line from the top of their head down through their waist, to their knees, and through the center of their feet. Their shoulders should push out as far as their bottom, while their chest pushes out as far as their toes.

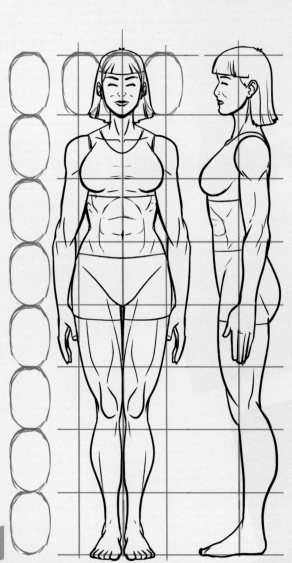

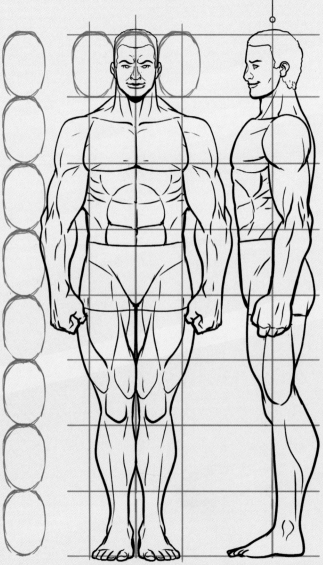

FACE TIME

Faces have their own proportions, with eyes and ears about halfway down the head. Here are average faces you can use for reference.

The ears are about the same height and position as the nose.

The eyes should be one eye-width apart.

Jaws are important to the shape of a person's face. They can be wide and square, narrow and sharp, or round and soft.

The nose forms an imaginary triangle with one point above the nose and one point on either side of the mouth.

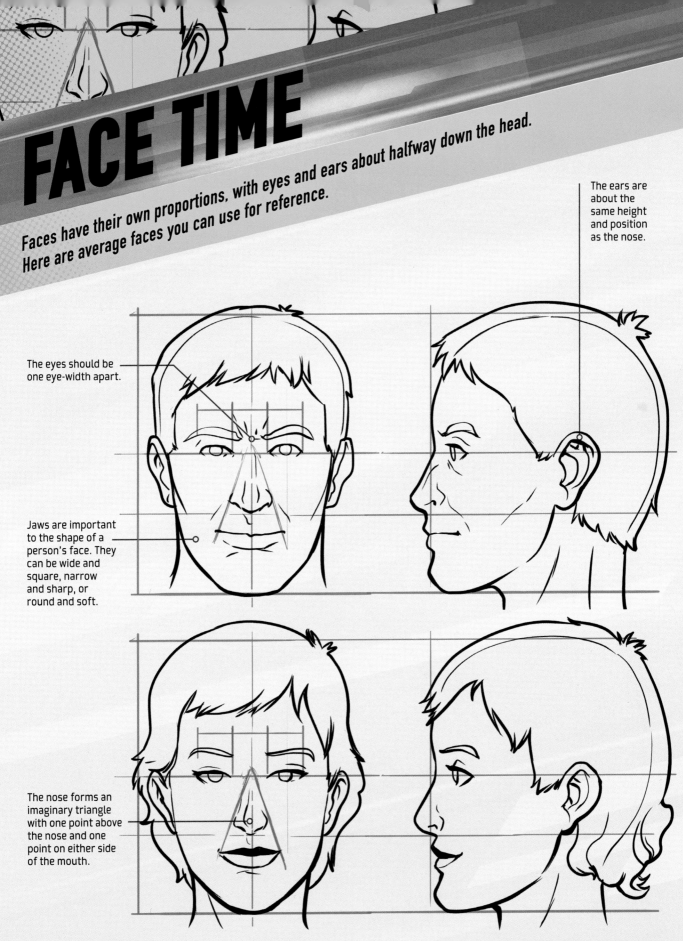

Look at your friends' and family members' faces. You will see many variations. Sketch the details you see and study their hairstyles. You can use traits like these to make each of your comic characters unique.

MAKING A MONSTER

In comic books, monstrous characters can be tragic heroes or terrifying villains. Here are some examples of both, and tips on how to create your own.

HARD AND SOFT

What weird powers will your monster have? The Concreature can turn his body from liquid to rock-hard concrete with a thought. To draw his body turning liquid, sketch a basic human shape, then add the folds and drips of the liquid parts over the top. Where his body is rock hard, his anatomy is more defined.

NAME: THE CONCREATURE

REAL IDENTITY: Vernon Klaas

POWERS: Able to turn his body into hard or soft concrete and increase his size to that of a four-story building.

ORIGIN: Following a betrayal, gangster Klaas was buried alive in the foundations of a chemical plant. A leakage altered his molecular structure, turning him into sentient concrete.

STRENGTH	◈◈◈◈◈
INTELLIGENCE	◈◇◇◇◇
SPECIAL POWERS	◈◈◈◈◇
FIGHTING SKILLS	◈◇◇◇◇

SOB STORY

A character who deserves sympathy is always more interesting than a mindless monster. The Concreature is trapped in his grotesque form, unable to properly resemble a human or mix with his former friends and family. This plight has made him an angry and pathetic creature.

HAIR-RAISING

Monstrous characters are often inspired by wild animals. Laughing Hyena is covered in bristly fur, like her namesake. When drawing fur, use a series of short lines that follow the shape of the body from the top of the head, down the back, and over the limbs. You should still see where the muscles are underneath the fur.

NAME: LAUGHING HYENA

REAL IDENTITY: Gina Rubio

POWERS: Ferocious strength, athleticism, and toxic bite.

ORIGIN: Bitten by a gene-spliced monster that had escaped from an illegal lab, stand-up comedian Rubio changed into a feral fighter.

STRENGTH ◆◆◆◇◇
INTELLIGENCE ◆◆◇◇◇
SPECIAL POWERS ◆◆◆◇◇
FIGHTING SKILLS ◆◆◆◇◇

WILD SIDE

It's not just the name and fur that makes Laughing Hyena seem feral and crazy. Her pose is animal-like; her grin and the way she holds her arms suggest a wild, slightly insane nature. Try to express your characters' personalities through their poses and facial expressions, even when they are not involved in the action.

BULKED UP

Megaton is an example of a muscle-bound character. His oversized arm muscles mean he can't bring them close to his body, so he takes up lots of space and seems even more imposing. A powerful figure like this is rarely seen in a relaxed pose. His hands are usually drawn as fists or in a gripping position.

NAME: **MEGATON**

REAL IDENTITY: **Samson Lepani**

POWERS: Can absorb impacts and deliver highly explosive punches.

ORIGIN: Fisherman Lepani was shipwrecked near a foreign atom-bomb test on Bikini Atoll, which caused him to mutate into a crazed human detonator.

STRENGTH ◇◇◇◇◇
INTELLIGENCE ◇◇◇◇◇
SPECIAL POWERS ◇◇◇◇◇
FIGHTING SKILLS ◇◇◇◇◇

CRACKING UP

Megaton has dark skin, which seems burned. Cracks appear in it, revealing the heat of a nuclear furnace just below the surface. It's almost as if he is bursting with power. A glow of green appears through the cracks to show the heat and energy within him.

LOOK SHARP

Though Barb has skin like a thorny lizard, she is human in shape. Draw Barb's anatomy first before adding spikes to her. Don't make them all point upward, but have each tiny triangle point outward from wherever it is sprouting on her body.

HERO OR VILLAIN?

Not every character can be defined as a hero or villain. Some may mean to be good but make mistakes that lead them down the wrong path. Though she once willingly worked for an evil scientist, Barb now feels anger at being turned into a "monster" and seeks **RETRIBUTION** and a cure. Her pose is awkward and defensive. She needs help, but has serious trust issues.

NAME: **BARB**

REAL IDENTITY: **Barbara Harrow**

POWERS: Has spine-firing, thorny skin.

ORIGIN: Assistant turned involuntary test subject of the evil genetics expert Dr. Sabine, Harrow has grown into a thorny, super-strong fighter with a spiky personality.

STRENGTH ◇◇◇◇◇◇
INTELLIGENCE ◇◇◇◇◇◇
SPECIAL POWERS ◇◇◇◇◇◇
FIGHTING SKILLS ◇◇◇◇◇◇

MAJOR MUSCLES

For the mightiest of heroes and villains, you have to look at bodybuilders to see similar anatomy. Here's how to bulk up your super-strong characters.

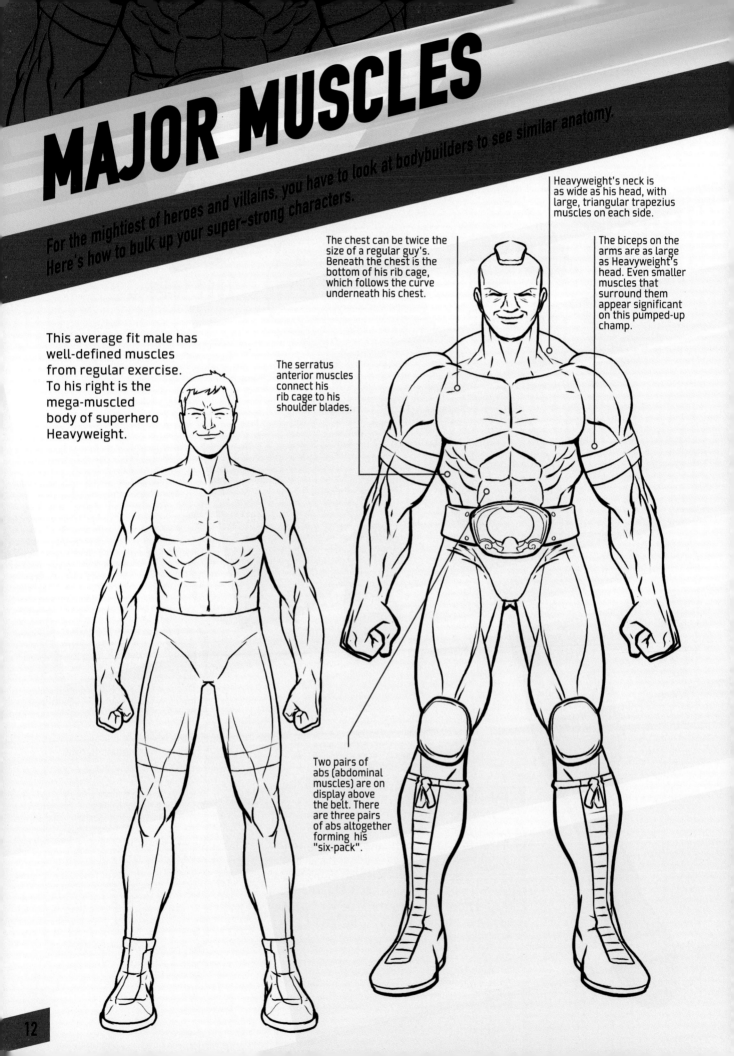

Heavyweight's neck is as wide as his head, with large, triangular trapezius muscles on each side.

The chest can be twice the size of a regular guy's. Beneath the chest is the bottom of his rib cage, which follows the curve underneath his chest.

The biceps on the arms are as large as Heavyweight's head. Even smaller muscles that surround them appear significant on this pumped-up champ.

This average fit male has well-defined muscles from regular exercise. To his right is the mega-muscled body of superhero Heavyweight.

The serratus anterior muscles connect his rib cage to his shoulder blades.

Two pairs of abs (abdominal muscles) are on display above the belt. There are three pairs of abs altogether forming his "six-pack".

TOP TIP

It may be tempting to add loads of made-up muscles to your super-strong heroes, but they will look much more convincing if you stick to exaggerating real ones.

NAME: HEAVYWEIGHT

REAL IDENTITY: Sean 'The Mass' Ducasse

POWERS: Able to control his own density to become a heavyweight hero.

ORIGIN: A radical xeta-ray treatment turned bodybuilder Ducasse into a super-dense mass of muscle.

STRENGTH	◆◆◆◆◇
INTELLIGENCE	◆◆◇◇◇
SPECIAL POWERS	◆◆◆◆◇
FIGHTING SKILLS	◆◆◆◇◇

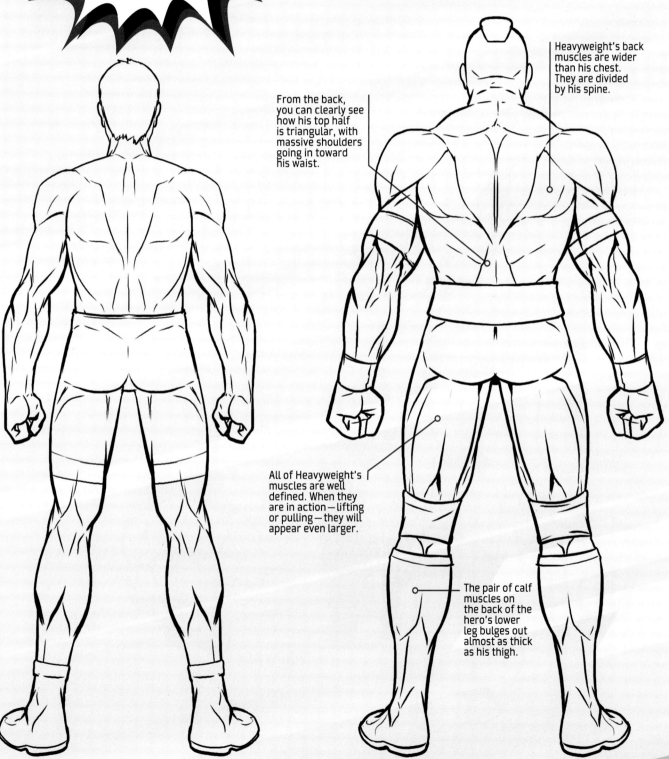

From the back, you can clearly see how his top half is triangular, with massive shoulders going in toward his waist.

Heavyweight's back muscles are wider than his chest. They are divided by his spine.

All of Heavyweight's muscles are well defined. When they are in action — lifting or pulling — they will appear even larger.

The pair of calf muscles on the back of the hero's lower leg bulges out almost as thick as his thigh.

TOUGH HIDES

Rock, fur, metal, and timber — here's how to give your towering titans some unusual skin types.

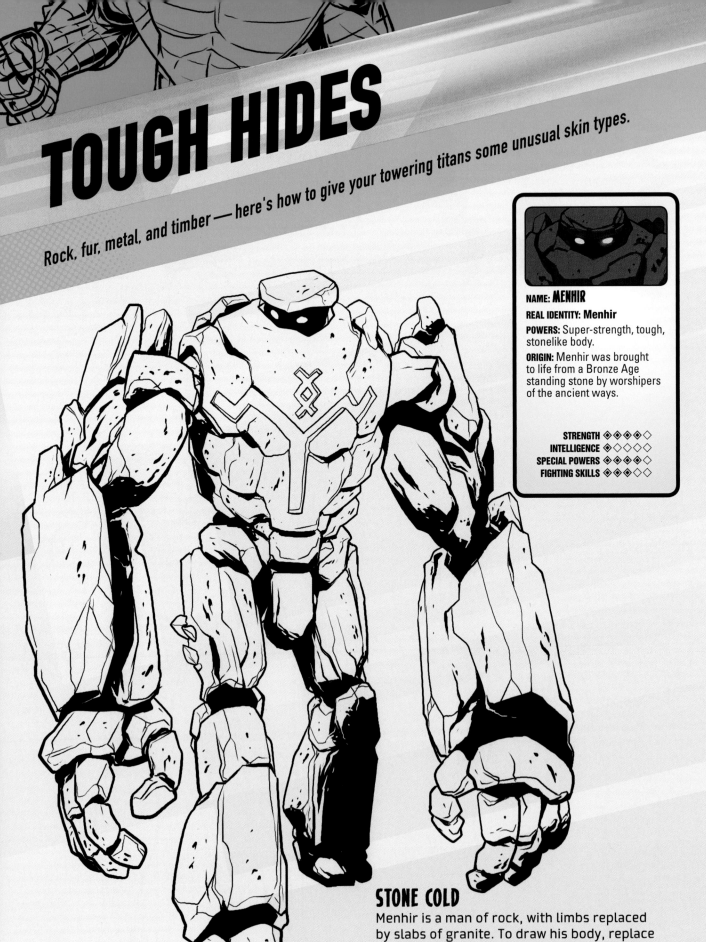

NAME: MENHIR

REAL IDENTITY: Menhir

POWERS: Super-strength, tough, stonelike body.

ORIGIN: Menhir was brought to life from a Bronze Age standing stone by worshipers of the ancient ways.

STRENGTH ◆◆◆◆◇
INTELLIGENCE ◆◇◇◇◇
SPECIAL POWERS ◆◆◆◆◇
FIGHTING SKILLS ◆◆◇◇◇

STONE COLD

Menhir is a man of rock, with limbs replaced by slabs of granite. To draw his body, replace human muscles with uneven, rocky shapes. Add a few thin cracks and scratches over the stones. When inking, leave a few spots and cracks showing in the shadows.

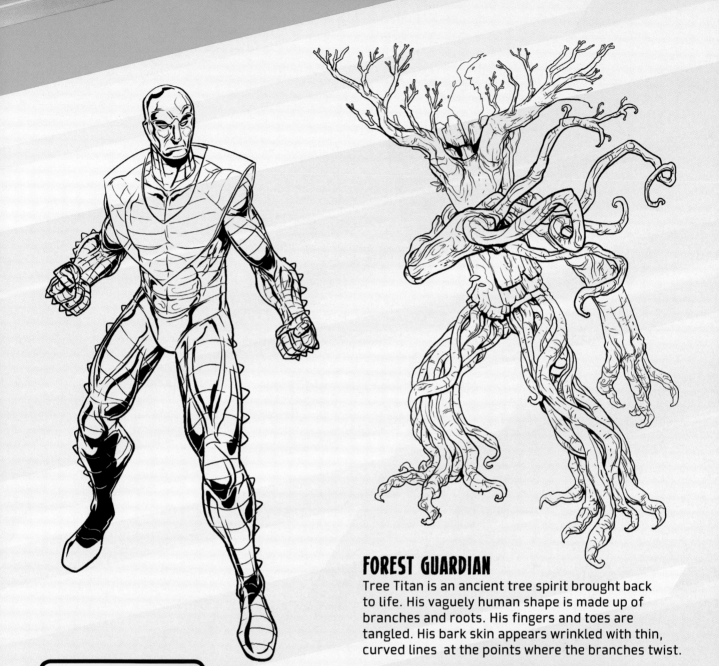

FOREST GUARDIAN

Tree Titan is an ancient tree spirit brought back to life. His vaguely human shape is made up of branches and roots. His fingers and toes are tangled. His bark skin appears wrinkled with thin, curved lines at the points where the branches twist.

NAME: STEEL MACE

REAL IDENTITY: Dr. Rachid Zafar

POWERS: Super-strength, tough steel-like body.

ORIGIN: Rogue scientist Zafar experimented with metals found on an alien world. He found a way to make liquid metal bond with his skin, making him bulletproof.

STRENGTH ◇◇◇◇◇
INTELLIGENCE ◇◇◇◇◇
SPECIAL POWERS ◇◇◇◇◇
FIGHTING SKILLS ◇◇◇◇◇

METAL MAN

For Steel Mace, the metal-skinned character, highlight the polish on his body by using thick, curvy lines that follow his muscle shapes. Break up these lines with a few semicircles to show where a light source reflects on him, with gaps between the segments on his skin.

NAME: TREE TITAN

REAL IDENTITY: "He who embodies the forest"

POWERS: Tree-like body can grow in size and produce strong, woody tendrils.

ORIGIN: The spirit of the South American forests has returned to punish those who destroy the natural world.

STRENGTH ◇◇◇◇◇
INTELLIGENCE ◇◇◇◇◇
SPECIAL POWERS ◇◇◇◇◇
FIGHTING SKILLS ◇◇◇◇◇

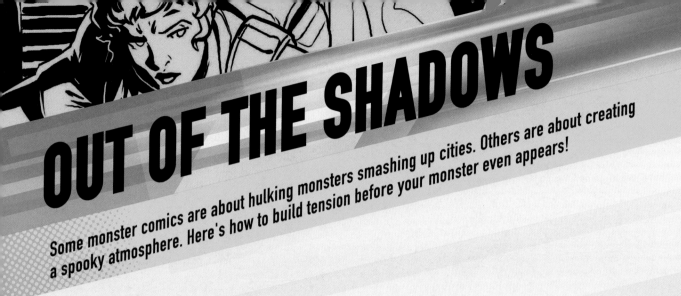

OUT OF THE SHADOWS

Some monster comics are about hulking monsters smashing up cities. Others are about creating a spooky atmosphere. Here's how to build tension before your monster even appears!

1. In this scene, monster hunter Elsa Nyberg is exploring a ruined crypt. It's a scary situation for sure, but how do you make the most of it? These pencil sketches do not make use of the light source.

TOP TIP
Position a light source to make the most of a spooky scene. Here, the low torchlight creates tall, black shadows on the walls. A light above would remove those.

2. The main light source is the flaming torch in Nyberg's hand. It lights up Nyberg's worried face from below and casts her shadow on the wall behind. Now the scene is more suspenseful.

3. In the finished ink drawings below, Nyberg's shadow looks like a creature creeping up on her. Highlights in the shadows pick out cracks in the wall, and the torn clothes and bones of the figure hiding in the alcove.

BODY LANGUAGE

How your characters stand can express as much about their personality or mood as their face or dialogue. Here are some poses that say a lot.

ARROGANT POSE

Corrosia is the ruler of the Dark Realm. You can tell she's the boss because of her **DOMINANT** stance — upright, with shoulders back, chin up, and chest out. She stands tall and looks down on those around her. Without her sneer, the same pose would work for the leader of a team of heroes.

NAME: QUEEN CORROSIA

REAL IDENTITY: Corrosia

POWERS: Her touch causes swift aging and decay.

ORIGIN: Mistress of the Dark Realm, Corrosia offers wealth and power in exchange for an early death.

STRENGTH ◈◇◇◇◇
INTELLIGENCE ◈◈◈◈◇
SPECIAL POWERS ◈◈◈◈◈
FIGHTING SKILLS ◈◇◇◇◇

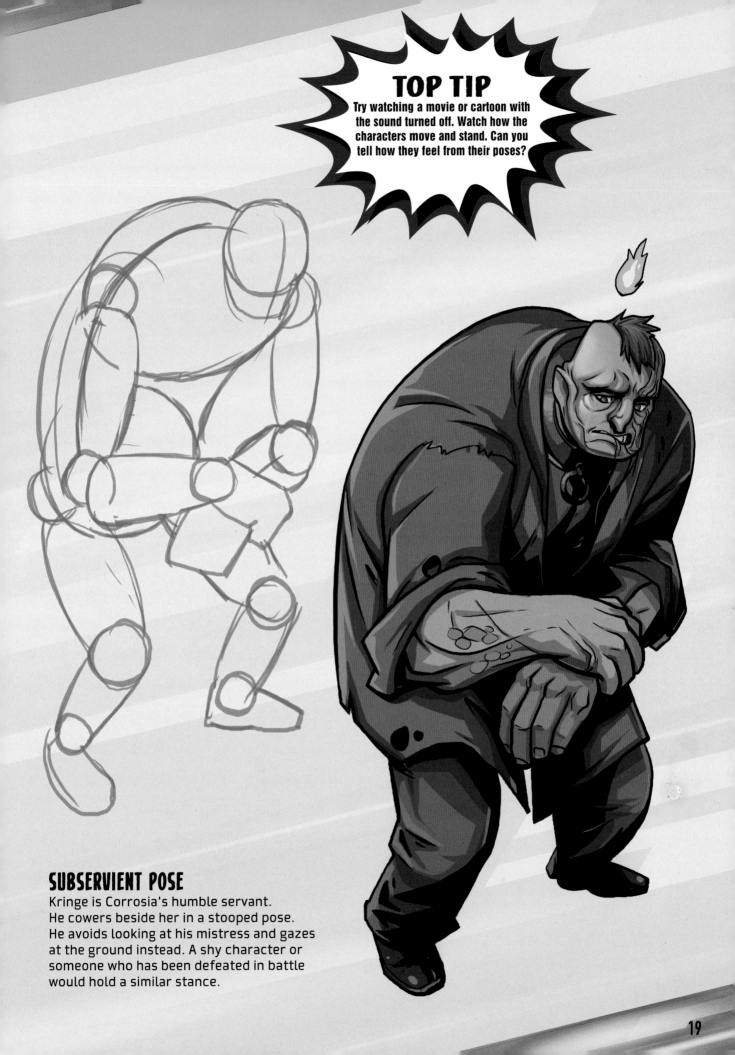

TOP TIP
Try watching a movie or cartoon with the sound turned off. Watch how the characters move and stand. Can you tell how they feel from their poses?

SUBSERVIENT POSE

Kringe is Corrosia's humble servant. He cowers beside her in a stooped pose. He avoids looking at his mistress and gazes at the ground instead. A shy character or someone who has been defeated in battle would hold a similar stance.

AGGRESSIVE POSE

From the pose, it's clear the Geckoid is not looking for friends. Dinner, maybe! He's leaning forward, raising his clawed, sticky hands, and waving his thorny tongue like a wild animal trying to frighten away intruders. This pose works for any tough character looking for a fight.

NAME: GECKOID

REAL IDENTITY: Eddie Marsh

POWERS: Super-strength, can cling to walls and ceilings, thorny, adhesive tongue.

ORIGIN: Sewage worker Marsh mutated into a monster after being bitten by a lizard that had been infected with pollutants.

STRENGTH ◆◆◆◆◇
INTELLIGENCE ◆◇◇◇◇
SPECIAL POWERS ◆◆◆◆◇
FIGHTING SKILLS ◆◇◇◇◇

TOP TIP

Keep your sketchbook handy to draw people in different poses. Your drawings don't have to be detailed — they just need to capture a natural gesture or a POSTURE.

TERRIFIED POSE

Eyes and mouth wide open, hands raised, body leaning backward — this guy looks scared, and you would, too, if you came across Geckoid! The body takes a defensive position when frightened, and leans away from the threat.

SPOOKY SETTINGS

Using different shading textures can add depth and atmosphere to your story settings. Practice using pens and brushes to match the marks used in these pictures.

Here are some different texture patterns you can use to shade your scary scenes.

TEMPLE RUINS

➤Ruins are great for **ATMOSPHERE**. This building looks like it has crumbled from centuries of neglect, or maybe a terrible event caused its destruction. A jungle setting suggests it is a lost temple full of mystery—and it's possibly still in use! Spooky statues, carvings, or unusual painted symbols can suggest a gruesome past.

MISTY FOREST

⌃For a spooky woodland scene, give the trees twisting branches that resemble arms and grasping claws. A mist weaving through the woods adds to the eerie mood. You can't see what's out there, but what you can see looks terrifying! A crow with bright white eyes seems to be spying on the **PROTAGONIST**.

DARE YOU ENTER . . . .

Following reports of nightly attacks, monster-slayer Simon Cleaver has traced large animal tracks to the abandoned home of the cursed Lord Lupei. But what is the best way to show his dramatic entrance?

NAME: SIMON CLEAVER

REAL IDENTITY: Simon Cleaver

POWERS: Immunity to vampire bites. Expert on monster killing.

ORIGIN: As a child, Cleaver saw both his parents killed by vampires. With a magical sickle that makes him immune to their bite, he swears to destroy all such monsters.

STRENGTH ◆◇◇◇◇
INTELLIGENCE ◆◆◆◇◇
SPECIAL POWERS ◆◇◇◇◇
FIGHTING SKILLS ◆◆◆◆◇

1. As the hero steps through the door, moonlight from outside casts his shadow inside the mansion. Though this symmetrical view is a good image, it is not the best dramatic angle. And with the hero and monsters mostly in silhouette, you can't see much detail.

2. This is a more exciting angle, with Cleaver and his sickle weapon in the foreground. But although we can see a monster hiding above him, we can't see how large or powerful it is. We need Cleaver to seem more in peril.

3. This is a better dramatic angle, looking down on the hero. You can see more of the monsters' shapes, with highlights picking out their details. From this angle, they also appear much larger than Cleaver.

THE HOUSE OF FEAR?

For the finished scene, a green tint was chosen to create a more supernatural atmosphere. Crosshatched inks have been used to build up the shadows and muscles on the monsters.

GRUESOME GALLERY

Why not invite some fearsome friends over for your monster-filled comic book story? Here are a few creepy characters you could introduce to your tale.

GARGOYLE

Once a stone sentinel over a church, the gargoyle has come alive to flap his batlike wings and spook anyone foolish enough to enter his turf at night. Add a dotted texture to his body to show that he is made of pockmarked stone.

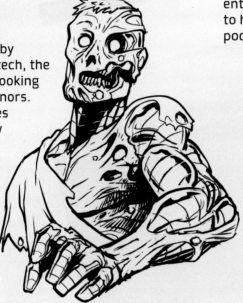

CYBER-ZOMBIE

Kept barely alive by transplants and tech, the cyber-zombie is looking for new organ donors. A few inky patches of darkness show where he needs some medical attention. Shade in his fleshy parts with fine lines to contrast with the shiny metal tech.

SWAMP CREATURE

The swamp has come alive in human form! Shade the patches of mud, moss, grass, and vines with crisscrossed lines that get thicker for the darker patches. This technique is called **CROSSHATCHING**.

WOLF MAN

The moon lights the wolf man from behind, leaving most of him in shadow. His fur is shaded with dashes that follow the shape of his muscles. Highlights reveal his torn shirt, bright eyes, and blood dripping from his fangs.

IDEAS BOARD

Never be stuck for inspiration for your comic books. Look around you, and keep notes and sketches in your own ideas book. Here are some images and phrases that could inspire characters and stories.

THE EVIL SIGNALMAN HAS TAKEN CONTROL OF ELECTRONICS, INCLUDING CAR GPS!

▸ Secret world trapped in a crystal. Prison planet or hostages?

TURN LEFT AT NEXT TURN... AND KILL!

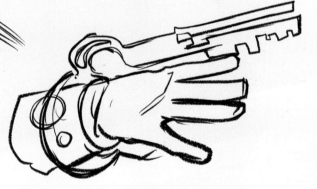

▲ Spylord's combination key can morph and unlock any door. What will he steal next?

▲ Earth's new owner arrives with plans to rebuild it from scratch.

▲ Amnesia has the power to steal memories! Will she discover the weapon launch codes?!

▲ Robot pests are multiplying!

29

TO BE CONTINUED . . .

Now it's over to you! We hope we've given you some ideas for stories and characters, and some good advice on how to create a professional-looking comic book story. But don't stop here — artists never stop learning!

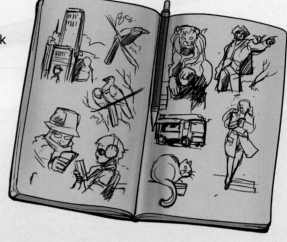

➤ Carry a small sketchbook with you at all times. You never know when an idea will hit. Draw every day, even if it's just a doodle.

◀ Read plenty, and not just comics. Books are full of ideas, too, with rich characters and situations.

◀ Show your work to friends, share your drawings online, and go to comic conventions to show your art to professionals. Comic pros can give you tips on how to improve your work.

➤ Movies are a great source of inspiration. Pay attention to the direction and movement of the camera, and the way light and shadows create mood.

GLOSSARY

ATMOSPHERE The feeling or mood that characters and readers experience in a certain location or situation.

CROSSHATCHING A way of creating shade using intersecting parallel lines.

DOMINANT More powerful.

POSTURE The way that the body is held.

PROTAGONIST The main character.

RETRIBUTION Hurting someone in the act of revenge.

TEXTURE The feel or appearance of a surface or substance.

FURTHER INFORMATION

Book to read

Create Your Own Monster by Magma Books (Laurence King, 2013)

Create Your Own Superhero Stories by Paul Moran (Buster Books, 2010)

DC Comics Coloring Book by DC Comics Warner Bros. (Studio Press, 2016)

Drawing Manga: Step by Step by Ben Krefta (Arcturus Publishing, 2013)

Drawing Monsters by Carolyn Scrace (Scribblers, 2015)

Stan Lee's How to Draw Superheroes by Stan Lee (Watson-Guptill, 2013)

Write and Draw Your Own Comics by Louise Stowell and Jess Bradley (Usborne, 2014)

Websites

PowerKids Press has developed an online list of websites related to the subject of this book. This site is updated regularly. Please use this link to access the list:
www.powerkidslinks.com/uca/monster

INDEX

Published in 2018 by **The Rosen Publishing Group, Inc.**
29 East 21st Street, New York, NY 10010

CATALOGING-IN-PUBLICATION DATA
Names: Potter, William.
Title: Drawing monstrous heroes / William Potter and Juan Calle.
Description: New York : PowerKids Press, 2018. | Series: Ultimate comic art | Includes index.
Identifiers: ISBN 9781508154730 (pbk.) | ISBN 9781508154679 (library bound) | ISBN 9781508154556 (6 pack)
Subjects: LCSH: Monsters in art--Juvenile literature. | Heroes in art--Juvenile literature. | Figure drawing--
    Technique--Juvenile literature. | Comic books, strips, etc.--Technique--Juvenile literature.
Classification: LCC NC1764.8.M65 P68 2018 | DDC 741.5'1--dc23

Copyright © 2018 Arcturus Holdings Limited

Text: William Potter
Illustrations: Juan Calle and Info Liberum
Design: Neal Cobourne
Design series edition: Emma Randall
Editor: Joe Harris

Manufactured in the United States of America
CPSIA Compliance Information: Batch BS17PK: For Further Information contact Rosen Publishing, New York, New York at 1-800-237-9932.